Gold

GOLD

FROM GREEK MYTH
TO COMPUTER CHIPS

RUTH G. KASSINGER

Material World

Twenty-First Century Books
Brookfield, Connecticut

To Ted, my 24-karat husband

Cover photograph courtesy of The Granger Collection, New York
Photographs courtesy of Scala/Art Resource, New York: pp. 4, 15, 17 (top), 24, 47, 68;
SuperStock: p. 6 (Egyptian National Museum, Cairo, Egypt/Bridgeman Art Library,
London); The Granger Collection, New York: pp. 9, 10, 61, 63; © Bettmann/Corbis: pp. 12,
22; North Wind Picture Archives: pp. 16, 28, 29, 52; Photofest: p. 34; Erich Lessing/Art
Resource, New York: pp. 17 (bottom), 36, 39; © Tom Pantages: pp. 48, 70; Photo
Researchers, Inc.: p. 55 (G. J. Hills, John Innes Institute/SPL); Photri-Microstock: p. 57;
Getty Images/Archive Photos: pp. 58 (Georgia Engelhard), 64 (Reuters/Peter Andrews), 69
(Reuters/STR). Map by Joe LeMonnier.

Library of Congress Cataloging-in-Publication Data
Kassinger, Ruth, 1954-
Gold / Ruth G. Kassinger.
p. cm. – (Material world)
Includes bibliographical references and index.
ISBN 0-7613-2110-1 (lib. bdg.)
Gold. I. Title.
QD181.A9 K37 2002   669'.22'09—dc21   2001042729

Published by Twenty-First Century Books
A Division of The Millbrook Press, Inc.
2 Old New Milford Road
Brookfield, Connecticut 06804
www.millbrookpress.com

*The Sumerians
made gold objects
of all kinds,
including these
vessels that date
back to 2450 B.C.*

Contents

Detail of a golden throne found in Tutankhamen's
tomb, depicting the boy pharaoh and his queen

CHAPTER ONE

The Ancient History of Gold

THE GOLD OF ANCIENT EGYPT

It was November 26, 1922, and the sun was baking the Egyptian desert to a shimmering 100° F (38° C). In a sloping passageway 30 feet (9 meters) beneath the desert sands, though, it was dark and cool. Archaeologists Howard Carter and Lord Carnavon and a team of English and Egyptian workers had just cleared the last of the debris from a door that had been sealed with plaster about 3,200 years earlier. Behind the door, they hoped, was the long-lost tomb of the Egyptian boy king, Tutankhamen.

For eight years, the team had been searching the ancient Egyptian burial grounds called the Valley of the Kings for King Tut's last resting place. Had they finally discovered it? The royal seals they found on the door bore his name. But would there be anything in the room behind the door? Or had tomb robbers, ancient and modern, plundered this tomb as they had robbed the tombs of nearly all the other ancient kings?

With trembling hands, Carter made a tiny hole in the upper left-hand corner of the door. He held a lit candle to the hole to see if any dangerous gases would snuff out the flame. The candle continued to burn. Carter widened the hole and then pushed the candle into the pitch-black room that lay behind the door. He peered in. At first, he could see nothing—air escaping from the interior made his candle's flame flicker and shrink. Then, gradually, as if from a dark mist, details emerged: "strange animals, statues, and gold—everywhere the glint of gold!"

The amount of gold in this first room of the tomb was staggering. Among the jumble of artifacts, three gold couches carved in the shape of beasts, a great gilt snake, and a pile of broken golden chariots caught Carter's eye. And against one wall, two life-size, jet-black statues of a king, clothed in Egyptian-style gold kilts and wearing gold sandals, guarded another sealed door.

Carter and his team were anxious to open the second door, but it took them about three months to carefully catalog and clear the first room. Finally, they entered the second chamber of the tomb, the burial chamber. The burial chamber was even more dazzling in its splendor than the first chamber. Four gold-covered shrines weighing about a half ton each, golden statues of goddesses, and an array of smaller golden objects glowed under the archaeologists' lamps. Most magnificent of all, though, were Tut's three coffins, one nested inside another. The outer coffin gleamed in a covering of gold foil. The middle coffin was overlaid with a sheet of gold that supported an intri-

Howard Carter, standing inside the sealed
burial chamber of King Tut

These gold, carnelian, and glass earrings, part of the vast treasure discovered in King Tut's tomb, feature enamel work separated by thin bands of gold.

cate mosaic of thousands of tiny pieces of red, turquoise, and black glass. The innermost coffin was made of solid gold, and it took eight men to lift it. Inside was Tut's mummified body, wrapped in gold.

King Tut's tomb is solid testimony to how deeply the ancient Egyptian royalty valued gold. But what was it about gold that made it so desirable? We're so accustomed to the idea that gold is valuable that the question seems odd. But, after all, gold is only a collection of a particular kind of metallic atoms.

Before about 4500 B.C., all people around the world lived directly off the land or sea, hunting, fishing, gathering wild plants, and sometimes farming. They lived in temporary settlements, and when the herds of wild animals they hunted made their annual migrations or when the soil no longer produced enough food, people moved on. People might stay in one area for a season or two, but they couldn't settle permanently.

Before about 4500 B.C., people certainly knew about gold, both alluvial gold, which washed down in streams, and ore gold, found in rocks near the earth's surface. No one at the time, though, had much interest in the metal. It was attractively shiny and made pretty beads in the small quantities people found, but it wasn't useful. Gold couldn't be used to make a knife or an ax blade because gold was too soft to hold a sharp edge. No one spent much energy collecting a material with so little practical value.

Some time between 5000 B.C. and 3500 B.C., in Egypt, in Mesopotamia (an area between the Tigris and Euphrates rivers, where Iraq is today), and in certain parts of Asia and Europe, people changed how they lived in an important way. These people learned how to fertilize and irrigate land, so it remained productive and they no longer had to find new land to farm after a few harvests. They domesticated wild cattle and goats, so they no longer had to follow migrating herds of animals to get a steady supply of meat. Now people could form permanent settlements.

At the same time, people began to fashion the first useful metal implements. They hammered copper into cups and shields. They covered their wooden plowshares with copper to make them more durable. By 3000 B.C., people had learned to make bronze, an alloy (mixture) of copper and tin that was considerably harder than copper.

Gradually, some people in these settled communities devoted less time to farming and began to specialize in crafts, such as pottery, metalwork, weaving, furniture making, tanning, dyeing, and boat building. These artisans traded the goods they made for the food they no longer grew themselves. They also tended to cluster near each other in the community, where their presence attracted other craftsmen, merchants, and traders. Towns developed and political organizations —headed by the families who controlled more land, livestock, or laborers than others—developed with them.

Around 3000 B.C., where the Nile River flows into the Mediterranean Sea, a prosperous family headed by a pharaoh (or king) united all the towns, villages, and farms of an area that was becoming known as Egypt. The power of the pharaohs and their descendants grew rapidly. The ruling pharaoh came to own all the land in Egypt and was regarded as a living god by his people.

During the Bronze Age, people cast molten metal to make a variety of tools and weapons.

There were vast deposits of gold in and near ancient Egypt. For the Egyptian rulers, the shiny but impractical metal known as *nub* had value. In ancient Egypt, people worshiped the life-giving, eternal sun. Gold, with its lustrous color and its rustproof, seemingly indestructible nature, seemed an earthly version of the sun. Pharaohs and members of the ruling family dressed in gold and surrounded themselves with gold objects to associate themselves with the sun. Only the pharaohs and their families had the right to use gold: It was an emblem of their divine and absolute power.

Gold mining in ancient Egypt was a horrible business. Gold miners in ancient Egypt were slaves, condemned criminals, and their families, and they labored underground in chains that prevented their escape. Men younger than thirty years old used picks to smash chunks from the rock walls, boys carried out the chunks that fell to the mine floor, and older men pounded them into small stones. Women and the oldest men ground the stones into powder. Once committed to the mines, miners might never see the light of day again. Most miners didn't live long: Death came from falling rocks, underground floods, arsenic fumes from fires used to crack rock, brutal heat, or exhaustion. Gold mining elsewhere in the ancient world was much the same.

Billions of years ago, when the Earth was young, gold and other metals and minerals in the Earth's core were melted by the great heat and pressure there. The molten (melted) materials, mixed with hot gases, were less dense than the surrounding rock, and gradually they rose toward the Earth's surface, squeezing between cracks in the rock. Over the eons, the rock shifted, and from time to time, some of these gold-filled cracks (called veins) were brought to Earth's surface. Then, streams rushing over the rock gradually wore it down and washed particles of gold downstream. Because gold is denser than water, the particles of gold sank to the stream bottoms.

The ancient Egyptians were lucky. They happened to be living near rich veins of gold, some of which the Nile River had been gradually eroding. The early Egyptians (roughly 4500 B.C. to 3000 B.C.) gathered the gold that could be easily sifted from water and sand. After they had gathered the surface gold, people had to dig trenches in the earth to uncover more of a vein. At first, the trenches they dug were shallow, but once they had retrieved the gold near the surface, they had to follow the veins deeper into the earth. The trenches became mines. Eventually, the Egyptian mines—all dug by hand with simple tools—would reach nearly 700 feet (215 meters) deep. That's as deep as a seventy-story building is tall.

GOLD AS ART

The splendor of the Egyptian rulers impressed people from neighboring countries, who also came to value gold as a sign of status and power. Rulers throughout the Middle East, South Asia, and the Mediterranean became extravagant in their use of gold. Some of these areas had no native gold, so rulers traded their country's products, such as wine, oil, fabric, spices, dyes, copper, and rare woods, for gold.

Much of the available gold was worn as jewelry or ornaments by royalty or was made into *gold foil* used to *gild* (cover) statues, furniture, and other objects in palaces and temples. The very qualities that made gold unsuitable for tools and weapons made it ideal for jewelry and ornaments. Gold can be hammered to nearly weightless foil, pulled into wires as thin as strands of hair, and molded into an endless variety of shapes.

The Egyptian artisans who fashioned jewelry and objects for the royal family enjoyed a high, almost priestly, status. They kept their techniques secret, revealing them only to those they chose to succeed them.

In Mesopotamia, where the Sumerians lived, *goldsmithing* (crafting jewelry and ornaments out of gold) developed later because the marshy land held no gold, and the Sumerians had to trade for Arabian and Egyptian gold. Their

ther than the fortunate find of Tutankhamen's tomb, most of what we know about Egyptian artistry in gold comes from representations in murals. Robbers stole almost all the gold objects from the pharaohs' tombs thousands of years ago.

This intricate golden helmet, found in the Sumerian city of Ur, dates back to 2450 B.C. and shows the talent of Sumerian goldsmiths.

artistry, however, was considerable. Around 2000 B.C., the wealthy Minoan kings on the Mediterranean island of Crete gathered gold in large quantities, and they, too, prized beautifully crafted jewelry. The Minoans exported their work and their goldsmithing techniques to Mycenae (which would become part of ancient Greece). Perhaps the most dazzling spectacle of gold in the ancient world, however, was King Solomon's Temple, built about 1000 B.C. in Jerusalem. According to legend, it was entirely covered in gold!

King Solomon's Temple
was an illustrious landmark of the ancient world, as depicted in this fanciful Renaissance drawing.

Ancient goldsmiths discovered many techniques for shaping gold that modern goldsmiths still use—hammering, bending, molding. Then to decorate it, they employed other techniques.

Repoussé, a technique of raising an area of the surface of a thin sheet of gold by pushing it from underneath, gave gold a sculptured look. Goldsmiths also decorated gold surfaces with tiny spheres of gold in a process called *granulation*, which involves soldering (joining two metals with another, heated metal). Sometimes they created gold *filigree* and soldered it onto gold or other metal objects, or even sewed it onto clothing. Gold filigree is made of tiny wires twisted and bent into fanciful, lacy designs.

A Mycenaean goldsmith used repoussé to create the raised figures on this gold cup in about 1500 B.C.

A goldsmith from Crete in the seventeenth century used granulation to decorate this bee pendant.

GOLD AS MONEY

When skilled artisans in Mesopotamia moved to town to make their living by their crafts, they traded their products for the food that farmers in the country produced. A potter who needed wheat might barter (exchange) some pots, for example, with a farmer who had grown extra wheat. They would bargain to arrive at a rate of exchange that satisfied both of them.

The barter system worked, but it was awkward. Suppose, for example, the wheat farmer had enough pots, but wanted honey. The potter might have to trade pots to a beekeeper for honey and then trade the honey to the wheat farmer. Finding the people with the right products to trade took time and patience. It was difficult, too, to determine prices. How many pots should a potter give up for a jar of honey? How much honey bought a sack of wheat? It was hard to know.

Money—any substance that everyone recognizes and accepts in exchange for goods—was needed. People used barley as money for a while, since everyone ate barley. But barley varied in quality, it was cumbersome to carry around, and eventually it would become moldy. In Mesopotamia, people experi-

The English word "money" comes from the name of the Roman goddess of warning, Moneta. In 390 B.C., the Romans stored their treasure in a temple dedicated to Jupiter. One day, so the story goes, when the Gauls were about to attack, the geese that lived near the temple started honking. Their honking alerted the Romans to the danger that threatened their gold. The grateful citizens built a shrine to Moneta, and the link between the rescued treasure and Moneta led, many centuries later, to the word for "money."

mented with silver as money. (Almost all the gold in ancient Egypt and Mesopotamia was owned by royalty.) Silver is instantly recognizable and, although it tarnishes (turns black) over time, it can be polished to its original luster. It is more abundant in the earth than gold, yet rare enough to be valuable. During the third millennium B.C., Mesopotamians increasingly paid for products and stored their profits in silver (and went back to cooking and eating their barley).

People paid for goods with an agreed upon amount of silver, which was determined by weight. At first, people formed their silver into rings or coiled bracelets and wore them. When they needed to buy something, they clipped off a bit, weighed it, and handed it over as payment. During the second millennium B.C., as more and more gold was discovered in Europe—where the rulers didn't monopolize it—gold, too, became money. By about 1000 B.C., scraps, lumps, bracelets, and rings of gold and silver passed freely and frequently from person to person and nation to nation.

There were problems, though, with using bits and pieces of silver and gold as money. It was a nuisance to weigh metal for every transaction. Sometimes, too, unscrupulous merchants or trading partners would cheat on the quantity or the quality of the metallic money. Merchants might use a balance (an early type of scale) that they had rigged to weigh in their favor. Or traders might mix a little of some less valuable metal in with the gold or silver that they presented as payment. Around 650 B.C., the kings of the ancient kingdom of Lydia first addressed these problems.

When you buy gold jewelry, you will often see the phrase "18 karat" on the label. A *karat* is a unit of purity equal to one part in 24. Pure gold is said to be 24 karat. An 18-karat gold ring is 18 parts gold and 6 parts another metal. Gold jewelry is often 18 karat or 14 karat because 24 karat is too soft to retain its shape well.

Sometimes you will see the purity of gold marked as a number, such as 999 pure. That means the gold is 99.9 percent pure. Sometimes the word "fine" is used instead of "pure."

Some pieces of gold jewelry are labeled *gold-filled*. This means the piece is made of another less-expensive metal (often silver) to which a layer of gold has been bonded. The term *gold-plated* and *gold-electroplated* apply to objects such as tableware that are only coated with gold.

Lydia was located at the eastern end of the Mediterranean Sea in present-day Turkey. Its capital city, Sardis, had the great fortune to be situated by the Pactolus River, which was rich with gold washed down from the mountains. Sardis was also well-placed for international trade. It became a central meeting point for traders arriving by land and sea from Europe, Asia, and Africa.

The people of Sardis grew wealthy from the gold in the Pactolus. (Actually, what they found in the Pactolus was an alloy of gold and silver called *electrum*.) They also became expert in money matters as they made exchanges among gold, silver, electrum, and goods for the many traders who came to trade in their city. To make these transactions easier, the many goldsmiths of Sardis began to form the bits and pieces of electrum into small, bean-shaped lumps called *dumps*.

Not all the goldsmiths' dumps were identical, so buyers and sellers still had to weigh each one. King Gyges (JI-jeez), who ruled Lydia in the late 600s B.C., decided he could improve the money system by forbidding individuals from making dumps. He decreed that only the government of Lydia could make dumps, which would all be an identical weight. Instead of weighing each dump, people could simply count out the needed number.

Next, King Ardys (AR-diss), who became king in 660 B.C., began to stamp the government-made dumps with a mark (a lion's head), so that people could see at a glance that their money had been issued by the government. If it was government-made, then people could be sure they had a coin with a certain weight. Within about fifty years, the bean-shaped dumps had come to look like our modern, identically stamped coins.

Finally, about 550 B.C., King Croesus (KREE-suss) had all the electrum coins melted down. Because gold and silver melt at different temperatures, the electrum separated into gold and silver. Then Croesus issued new coins, either pure gold or pure silver, of various weights, stamped them, and declared that one gold coin of a particular weight was worth ten silver ones of the same weight. The world had a modern currency.

Those reforms meant that gold and silver no longer had to be weighed. But what about the purity, particularly of gold? The Lydians had an answer for that problem, too. A local black stone, called a *touchstone*, some Lydian discovered, could test the purity of a piece of metal that was said to be gold. When a goldsmith rubbed a piece of gold against a touchstone, it left a streak. The goldsmith then compared the color of the streak to a set of twenty-four needles. Twenty-three needles contained varying, known mixtures of gold, silver, and copper. The last needle was pure gold. By matching the streak on his black touchstone with one of his needles, a skilled goldsmith could determine whether the "gold" was pure and, if not, what its real composition was.

GOLD AND WAR

Persia (modern Iran) invaded Lydia in 546 B.C., and all the Lydian wealth fell to the Persians. The Persians adopted the Lydian idea of gold coinage, too, and established their own *mint*. (A mint is where money is manufactured.) Gold, once owned only by royalty, had become so common as currency that the Persian government collected gold coins from its citizens as payment for taxes.

However, Persian royalty did not neglect the traditional use of gold as a demonstration of royal wealth and power. Darius, the Persian "King of Kings," surely awed his troops with the golden chariot, the golden throne, and the golden bathtub that traveled with him on his military campaigns!

A gold "alexander" coin

When Alexander the Great, king of Macedonia and Greece, went on his great military campaigns to conquer Persia, Egypt, and Babylon between 336 and 326 B.C., he needed money. His troops were mostly mercenaries (soldiers from other countries who fought for pay rather than out of patriotism), and Alexander paid their salaries in gold coins. Hoping to prevent the mercenaries from looting conquered cities, he also gave them gifts of gold coins. (His troops still looted, but perhaps not as much as they might have.) The coins he had minted, which included gold melted down from the treasures he captured, were stamped with his famously handsome profile. These gold "alexanders" circulated for 150 years, advertising far and wide the power of Greece.

Gods and goddesses assembled on Mount Olympus
with Zeus presiding at the top. From a nineteenth-century
ceiling painting in Florence, Italy

CHAPTER TWO

Myth, Magic, and Gold

GOLD AND THE GREEK GODS

There was little gold to be found in the earth in Mycenae, the birthplace of Greek culture. The Mycenaeans, though, were familiar with—and envious of—the gold of their neighbors. To the north, gold washed down the rivers of Macedonia and Thrace. To the south, the Minoan kingdom on the island of Crete was a major sea power and trading center, and its goldsmiths crafted beautiful gold objects for the Minoan royalty. And to the east lay the powerful Hittite Empire (part of modern Turkey), already tapping the alluvial gold found in the mountain streams that would, a thousand years later, make the Lydians rich.

Many of the familiar ancient Greek myths about the gods and heroes evolved in Mycenae between 1600 and 1300 B.C. In these myths, which circulated as spoken stories for hundreds of years before people began to write them down, Zeus and his fellow gods live in golden palaces on Mount Olympus, drink from golden goblets, and sit in golden chairs. Hera, wife of Zeus, wears golden sandals, Apollo crosses the sky every day in a golden chariot, and Cupid shoots golden arrows to inspire love. Only gods, the Mycenaeans imagined, would use precious gold in such extravagant ways.

In one Greek myth, Zeus even becomes gold. According to the story, Acrisius, king of Argos, is terrified by a prophecy that his young daughter, Danaë, will one day have a child who will kill him. In order to foil the prophecy, when Danaë becomes a young woman, Acrisius locks her in a bronze tower. Unfortunately for Acrisius, Zeus, looking down from Mount Olympus, sees the beautiful young woman. He turns himself into a shower of gold and falls, like rain, upon Danaë.

As a result of Zeus's golden encounter with Danaë, the hero Perseus is born. When Perseus grows up, he kills the dreaded snake-haired Medusa, who turns all who look on her to stone. Fate is never denied, though, in Greek mythology: Perseus accidentally kills his grandfather, Acrisius, in a discus-throwing competition.

In one powerful old myth, gold lies at the heart of life and death. The story starts when Phryxus and Helle, son and daughter of a king, want to escape from their nasty step-mother. The two siblings flee on the back of a winged ram with fleece of pure gold, which had been a gift from the god Hermes to their mother before she died. Helle slips off and falls into the sea, but Phryxus arrives safely in Colchis, a kingdom far from Greece on the shores of the Black Sea. In gratitude to Hermes and anxious for the friendship of Æetes, whose kingdom he has landed in, Phryxus sacrifices the ram to Zeus and gives the golden fleece to Æetes. Æetes is overjoyed with the gift because an oracle has told him that his life depends on having just such a fleece, and he sets a dragon to guard it.

Back in Greece, sometime after Phryxus's escape, a young man named Jason appears before King Pelias to assert his father's claim to Pelias's throne. Pelias agrees to give up the throne, with only one small condition: that Jason fetch him the Golden Fleece. Jason convinces fifty sons of gods and goddesses to sail with him on his ship, the *Argo,* on this great adventure. With the help of the goddess Hera and his crew, Jason overcomes rocks and other obstacles to arrive safely at Colchis.

In Colchis he meets Medea, the daughter of Æetes. When Medea sees Jason, she is struck by one of Cupid's golden arrows and immediately falls in love with him. With her magical powers—and a promise from Jason of marriage—she betrays her father and sings the dragon to sleep so that Jason can steal the fleece. But after their return to Greece, Jason betrays Medea, leaving her in order to marry a daughter of King Creon of Corinth instead.

A golden ram may seem like an odd form of transportation, but there was a reason for it. The ancient Greeks used fleece (the unsheared hide of a sheep) to pan for gold in fast-flowing streams. The thick curls of the fleece trapped the heavy specks of gold and let the lighter sand pass through. For people who saw a gold-flecked fleece, it was easy to imagine the golden ram it must have come from!

Jason's ship, the Argo, *sets sail on its quest for the Golden Fleece.*

Adding insult to grievous injury, Jason offers Medea a quantity of gold as solace for her disappointment. Medea doesn't take such treatment lightly. She spins the gold into cloth, sews it into a gown, drenches the gown in a magical poison, and then gives it to Jason's bride as a wedding present. The young woman slips into the gown with delight, only to die in agony.

GOLD AND THE SCANDINAVIAN GODS

The region of northern Europe called Scandinavia has few natural gold deposits, so the metal was rare and highly prized. Until the Vikings went on their famous plunderings across Europe starting in the eighth century A.D., only the wealthiest of Scandinavians had gold. The Scandinavians, like the early Greeks, naturally imagined gold as a material fit for the gods. In Norse mythology, Frey, the god of fertility, rides a golden

The Vikings sailed from as far away as Denmark to raid the English and other peoples of Europe.

boar across the summer sky. His boar's golden bristles are the rays of the sun, lighting up the dark and increasing the harvests. The gods eat golden apples that keep them eternally young. The most beautiful and beloved of the Norse gods is Balder. His golden locks glow like beams of sunlight, and he is worshiped as the radiant god of innocence and light.

One of the most powerful Norse gods is Thor, the thunder god. Thor's wife, Sif, is noted for her beautiful, long golden hair. One day, so the story goes, a mischievous god named Loki sneaks into the bedroom of Thor and Sif and cuts off all of Sif's beautiful hair. When Thor wakes the next morning and sees what Loki has done, Thor threatens to break every bone in Loki's rascally body if he doesn't find a way to restore Sif's hair. A desperate Loki flatters the evil-tempered but clever gnomes into helping him out. The gnomes draw magic circles, mumble spells and incantations, and finally spin new hair for Sif—out of real gold. The hair takes root and Sif becomes truly golden-haired, "as fitted the wife of the great Thor."

GOLD AND MORTALS

In the early Greek myths, gold in the hands of the gods is a source of beauty and usually, like Hermes's golden ram and Apollo's golden chariot, of good. But gold in the hands of mortals, like Medea, can be a source of evil. A much later Greek myth, which arose when the Greeks were wealthier, demonstrates how gold in the hands of people can lead to grief.

The story takes place in Phrygia, a kingdom ruled by Midas. One day the king's gardeners come upon a satyr (a half-goat, half-man follower of the god Dionysus) in a drunken stupor in the king's gardens. The gardeners bind him up and deliver him to the king. When the satyr awakens, he entertains the king with eye-opening stories about the world beyond Phrygia. After a few days, the king kindly assigns a guide to lead the satyr back to Dionysus. Dionysus, who had been worried about the satyr, calls on Midas to ask him how he would like to be rewarded for his good deed. The king replies, "Pray grant that all that I touch be turned into gold."

Dionysus grants his wish, and Midas delights in turning his house, his clothes, his cup and bowl, and many other household objects into gold. But when he finds that food and water also become gold in his hands and his daughter turns to gold in his arms, he begs to be released from his wish. Dionysus, who, after all, is the god of pleasure, laughingly agrees and tells him to go wash in the nearby river. King Midas obeys. To his relief, his golden touch washes away . . . into the waters of the Pactolus River. From that day forward, gold was found in the sands of the Pactolus.

In 1957 archaeologists uncovered the tomb of Midas. In the tomb were numerous bowls, plates, and cups that had contained food and drink from the elaborate feast held at Midas's burial about 700 B.C. In the late 1990s, archaeologists scraped the dinnerware and performed chemical analyses of the residues. They were able to determine exactly what the mourners ate (a stew made of barbecued lamb and lentil beans spiced with fennel) and drank (a beer/wine/honey mixture). In September 2000, the University of Pennsylvania Museum, which had supported the research, hosted a dinner that was a re-creation of the burial feast held 2,700 years earlier.

King Midas was a real person who ruled a real kingdom called Phrygia (an area of modern western Turkey bordering the Aegean Sea) in about 700 B.C. Phrygia was not a part of Greece, but its people spoke a language related to Greek and traded regularly with the Greeks. The Phrygians, like their neighbors the Lydians, found great deposits of gold in the streambeds of the Pactolus River, which ran through both countries.

The myth explains why the Pactolus ran with gold. But it also warns listeners of the consequences of loving gold excessively. By the time this myth developed, gold was common as coinage, and greed had apparently become an all too common problem in prosperous Greece.

Gold and greed were also on the mind of another famous Phrygian: the master storyteller Aesop. Aesop, who lived two hundred years after Midas in the sixth century B.C., was of Ethiopian heritage and was likely a slave in Phrygia. (His name may have been a corruption of his birthplace, Ethiop.) In his fable *The Goose That Laid the Golden Egg,* a married couple find that their goose lays a golden egg every morning. This leads them to suppose that the goose must have a great lump of gold inside. Not satisfied with one golden egg per day, they decide to kill the goose to get the big lump inside. When they look inside, though, they discover she's like any other goose. In their greediness for more, the pair lose what they already have.

A MODERN TALE OF GOLD

Aesop was a moralist: He told his stories to convey a lesson. Lyman Frank Baum, author of *The Wizard of Oz* and many other books, was a storyteller in the tradition of Aesop. *The Wizard of Oz* is not only a great adventure story for kids, it can also be read as a parable. (A parable is a story designed to illustrate a moral truth or principle by using symbolic characters.) Baum, who lived much of his adult life in the midwestern United States, wrote about gold and silver in the lives of midwesterners in the last decades of the 1800s.

The United States at the end of the nineteenth century was on the *gold standard,* which meant anyone could bring a dollar to a bank and receive a dollar's worth of gold, at a fixed rate, in exchange. At the same time, American farms were in trouble. Prices for the products of many midwestern and some southern farmers were falling. Farmers couldn't earn enough to pay back their loans, and bankers were seizing and selling farms to recover the loans they had made to farmers.

Many midwestern and southern farmers blamed their troubles on the gold standard. They recalled better times, and those better times were before 1873, when dollars could be exchanged for *either* gold or silver. They came to believe that the gold standard was bankrupting them. If only dollars could be freely converted to silver as well as gold, the farmers concluded, their troubles would be over. They wanted dollars to be convertible to silver because there was a lot of silver available. Silver convertibility would lead to inflation. Inflation would make it easier for farmers to repay their loans to the banks.

You can read Baum's *The Wizard of Oz* as a midwesterner's parable of the evils of the gold standard. Dorothy, who comes from a Kansas farm, stands for honest, kind, and trusting mid-

Dorothy and her friends take the yellow brick road to the
Emerald City, home of the great Wizard of Oz.

westerners who want—like Dorothy—only to stay on their farms. When Dorothy is thrown off her farm, she is told to follow the yellow brick road—which symbolizes gold—to find the answer to her problem. The path of gold, though, leads to the powerful, but humbug, Wizard of Oz. The Wizard symbolizes bankers who support the gold standard and oppose adding silver to it. The Wizard pretends to help Dorothy, but actually sends her off on a mission that could kill her. In the farmers' minds, the bankers were hurrying them to economic death. At the end of the book, the Wizard is forced to admit he is a fraud. Only Dorothy's *silver* slippers can take her home to Kansas.

As you'll see in Chapter Five, you can no longer take your dollar bills (or Mexican pesos, British pounds, or most other currencies) into a bank and exchange them for gold. Gold sells for less than platinum and other rarer or more useful metals. Many people, not just the very wealthy, can afford to own gold jewelry. But gold still is a symbol with deep meaning in our culture. Would it be so thrilling to win a first-place tin medal at the Olympics? Would an actress kiss an iron Oscar with such feeling? Would you be reassured to see a "lead seal of approval" on a product? The lustrous metal of the gods still dazzles our eyes and sparks our imaginations.

The producers of the movie version of *The Wizard of Oz* changed Dorothy's slippers from silver to ruby when they discovered that silver didn't show up well on film.

Aristotle, at the top, converses with Alexander
the Great in this fresco in a government building, Paris, France.
Note the beautiful gilded parts of the ceiling.

CHAPTER THREE

Making Gold

When Alexander the Great conquered Egypt in 332 B.C., he introduced not only his Greek gold coins to the Egyptians but also some unique ideas about gold. Alexander was greatly influenced by the famous Greek philosopher Aristotle, who had been his childhood tutor. Aristotle taught some revolutionary ideas about the nature of matter, including gold, that found an interested audience in Egypt.

Aristotle was a great observer of nature and drew conclusions about how the world works from his observations. One of the general trends that Aristotle noticed was that immature (and in Aristotle's view, valueless) beings grow into mature (valuable) beings. For example, useless seeds grow into edible plants, helpless lambs grow into wool-bearing sheep, and unreasoning babies grow into rational adults. Generalizing from his observations, Aristotle concluded that all things in this world—plants, animals, and people—grow toward perfection.

Aristotle thought his theory applied to metals, too. He observed that there were large amounts of unattractive (or "base") metals, such as tin, lead, and iron, in the ground. Copper, an attractive metal, was harder to find than these other, uglier metals, and silver (which seemed more attractive to him than copper) was rarer still. He concluded that copper, which corroded easily, and silver, which tarnished, actually started as one of the base metals and were still in the process of maturing into gold. Gold was the perfection of all metals because it was the rarest and because nothing could destroy it or even dull its glow.

Aristotle had another idea about matter. He, like other Greeks of his time, believed that all materials in the physical world were made of four elements: earth, air, water, and fire. It was the proportion of the four elements in any material that gave the material its properties. Although Aristotle never tried to prove it, he predicted that one material could be transformed into another by altering the mix of its elements.

When Aristotle's two ideas reached Egypt through Alexander, they excited the imagination of certain Egyptian artisans. Egypt had some of the world's finest goldsmiths, as well as the world's most technically advanced glassblowers and dyers. These were people who were adept at chemical transformations. Certain artisans reasoned that if they could turn

Aristotle's belief about the four elements was based, in part, on his observations of burning wood. Ignited wood, he believed, returned to its four elements: ash (earth), smoke (air), steam (water), and fire.

Egyptian goldsmiths use special tools to create golden urns and vessels. From a wall painting in the tomb of a royal official, Luxor-Thebes, Egypt

sand and a few other ordinary ingredients into beautiful glass and transform ugly plant roots into gorgeous dyes, why shouldn't they turn ugly, common lead into beautiful gold? Aristotle, already famous and revered, had said it was possible. In fact, he had said that it happened all the time under the ground, just very slowly. All a craftsman had to do, these Egyptians reasoned, was speed up the natural process.

The Egyptian craftsmen started to practice *alchemy,* the would-be science of turning metals and other materials into gold. These early alchemists sometimes thought their experiments had succeeded. One ancient Egyptian recipe for "diplosis" (doubling) of gold called for heating a mixture of two parts gold with one part each of silver and copper. Indeed, if you tried the recipe today, the result would be twice as much of a lovely golden material. Actually, though, the material wouldn't be gold, but a gold, silver, and copper alloy. Because the silver gives the material a greenish tint and the copper gives it a reddish tint, mixing both with gold hardly changes the color of the original gold.

The problem for the early alchemists was that they didn't know exactly what gold was. Gold found in nature often is combined in alloys, so the standard for gold was murky. For some early alchemists, if a metal looked like gold, it was gold.

Later, alchemists used the touchstone (see Chapter One) to verify that a substance was pure gold. *Cupellation* was another way to test gold. Alchemists put the material they hoped was on its way to becoming gold into a porcelain cup (called a *cupel*). The cupel would absorb any impurities and, if there was gold in the material, there would be a pure gold button at the bottom of the cupel.

Sometimes, though, cupellation fooled alchemists. They would subject some molten lead, for example, to various alchemical procedures and then test it with cupellation. Lo and behold, the lead would disappear into the cupel and the tiniest bit of gold would appear at the bottom! The alchemists would announce with delight and sincerity that they were on the path to success. What really happened was that the piece of lead already had microscopic specks of gold in it. Cupellation simply amassed the invisible specks into one barely visible bit.

As Egyptian alchemists found that transformation by heating, mixing, and other mechanical and chemical means didn't work, they became increasingly secretive and mystical about their efforts. They began to focus greater attention on Aristotle's idea that metals are living beings. If they could isolate the soul of gold and transfer it to another metal, they hypothesized, then the second metal would become gold. Zosimos, an Egyptian who lived about A.D. 300, and other alchemists of the time had visions and dreams that they believed explained the secrets of alchemy. A mysterious author named Trismegistus produced works declared to be the words of Thoth, the Egyptian god of wisdom. Alchemy moved far from its empirical (guided by experiment) roots and into the realm of magic.

Zosimos and other alchemists wrote down their visions and dreams in a complex language that used symbols to represent materials and processes. They looked to myths, which they

Ancient Egyptian goldsmiths and others who practiced alchemy believed that silver, mercury, and sulfur were the most likely substances to be transformed into gold. Aristotle had written that silver was just one step from gold. Mercury, too, had a silvery color. In addition, mercury is a metal that is liquid at room temperature and forms balls that skitter away at a touch. Alchemists assumed that mercury was therefore alive and would quickly grow into gold. Sulfur is bright yellow (which alchemists thought was nearly gold). Sulfur also seemed alive because it easily bursts into flame.

believed contained hidden, secret recipes for making gold, for many of their symbols. Instead of writing "gold," they would draw a symbol for the sun because gold and the sun were linked in Greek mythology. Instead of writing "silver," they might draw a moon or write "Artemis," the Greek goddess of the moon. Other gods and goddesses represented iron, copper, and lead.

When the Romans conquered Egypt in the first century A.D., they were suspicious of alchemy and suppressed it. Diocletian, the Roman emperor from A.D. 284 to 305, ordered that all alchemical writings be destroyed because he feared that his rebellious subjects might make gold and use it to fund an uprising. When the emperor Constantine made Christianity the official religion of the Roman Empire about ten years later, he forbade the study of pagan (meaning non-Christian and non-Jewish) ideas, including alchemy.

The ancient Chinese were also intrigued with alchemy, although they were more interested in achieving immortality than gaining great riches. Because nothing seemed able to destroy gold, people thought that if they could incorporate gold into their bodies, their bodies would likewise continue unchanged forever. Simply eating gold didn't do the trick, so Chinese alchemists tried to manufacture a gold that would ensure immortality.

An alchemist to the court of the first Chinese emperor (about 206 B.C.) convinced the emperor to swallow potions containing mercury. The emperor died (mercury is a potent poison), but that unfortunate outcome didn't stop several later emperors from trying similar potions . . . with similar results. Why didn't these tragedies put an end to this kind of alchemy? Scholars suggest that because the emperors' corpses were laced with mercury, they decomposed more slowly than usual. It may have seemed to observers that the alchemists had achieved a partial success.

In A.D. 634 the Arab followers of the prophet Muhammad embarked on a course of conquest to spread their new religion of Islam. The Arab empire, which eventually stretched from South Asia (where Pakistan is today) through the Middle East and North Africa to Spain, would last for centuries. The Muslims, as followers of Islam were called, were intellectually curious and open-minded about science. The city of Baghdad (in modern Iraq) became a center of learning, where scholars from India, Egypt, and Arabia gathered. Arab scholars translated many rare Egyptian and Greek medical, alchemical, and scientific texts into Arabic. Using these works as a basis, a new generation of alchemists experimented with various metals and chemicals, hoping to uncover the secrets of gold. Although they failed to produce gold, Arab alchemists made remarkable progress in discovering and classifying the properties of a wide range of chemical materials.

Europeans knew little of developments in the Arab world for more than four hundred years. Not until crusaders attempted to conquer Jerusalem in about A.D. 1100 did Europeans encounter alchemy. When the crusaders took this strange so-called science of alchemy back to Christian Europe with them, the Catholic Church no longer condemned alchemy for its pagan roots. By this time, church leaders had adapted the ideas of pagan Aristotle so that they conformed to Christian thought. The fact that the great Aristotle had written that base metals might be transformed into gold made alchemy an acceptable, even respectable, profession.

Medieval European kings and princes were overjoyed to hear about alchemy. Much of the trade of the world was carried out with the exchange of gold coins by this time, so there was a huge demand for gold. European royalty eagerly hired alchemists and set them up in elaborate laboratories.

Some alchemists honestly believed that they could make gold. Bernard Trevisan, an Italian born of a prosperous and noble family in 1406, was typical. He devoted his life to reading the old texts and concocting recipes based on his understanding of the cryptic directions in the texts. In one typical experiment, he dissolved silver and mercury in a strong acid, heated the solution until it was reduced by half, and then exposed the solution to the sun's rays. "For does not the sun acting upon and within the earth form metals?" he asked. "Is not gold merely its beams condensed to a yellow solid?" Poor Trevisan worked with this particular mixture for five years before giving up. Trevisan lived to be nearly ninety years old, spent his fortune on alchemy, and died still dreaming of making gold.

In the process of their work, medieval alchemists developed some excellent laboratory techniques and equipment that would serve chemists of the future well. They also manufactured some powerful new substances, including a combination of nitric and hydrochloric acids that they called *aqua regia.* Aqua regia dissolves gold. You might think this would have made alchemists wonder if gold really was the perfect metal. The alchemists reasoned otherwise. If they could dissolve gold, they thought, then surely they would be able to create it!

Some alchemists were simply swindlers who played on uneducated people's wishful thinking. Like con artists today, they had a number of techniques for fooling the gullible. One trick involved a special crucible (a pot for heating mixtures) with a false bottom, which contained a hidden gold coin. The swindler would drop a potential customer's silver coin into such a crucible full of an alchemical mixture that would supposedly turn the coin into gold. He then stirred the concoction, lifted the false bottom, and released the gold coin into the mixture. After some time, he fished out the gold coin and gave it to the astonished observer.

Here's another trick that fooled people. A dishonest alchemist would make a big show of dipping what looked like a dark iron nail into a crucible filled with an alchemical liquid. When the nail was pulled out—presto!—it had turned into gold.

One prince, Frederick of Wurtzburg, had a special gallows painted in gold, which he used only to dispatch alchemists who failed to produce gold. On the gallows were these words: "I once knew how to fix mercury and now I am fixed myself." This saying is a clever play on two meanings of the word "fix." Alchemists "fixed" mercury by changing it from a liquid to a solid. (Alchemists thought "free" mercury would turn into gold more quickly.) The other meaning of "fix" is "fasten." So, the unfortunate alchemist who knew how to fix mercury is now fixed (that is, fastened) to the gallows and is unable to escape his fate.

In reality, the nail was already gold! The swindler had painted it black beforehand to resemble iron, and an acid in the alchemical liquid dissolved the paint.

After such demonstrations, some gullible people would hand over more of their silver to be turned into gold. (A gold coin was about ten times more valuable than a silver one.) The alchemist would warn that he would need a day or two to transform such a large quantity of silver. After collecting the silver, the alchemist quickly left town. This was a dangerous game, however. Many a dishonest (or simply failed) alchemist was hanged or burned at the stake.

As incredible as alchemy is to us today, it seemed perfectly logical to many people of medieval times and earlier. After all, before people had any real understanding of science, they witnessed all sorts of inexplicable transformations. Grape juice turned into wine, water disappeared into thin air, iron turned to rust, and eggs turned into chickens. Why shouldn't lead turn into gold?

A belief in alchemy wasn't limited to greedy kings and uneducated peasants. As late as the 1600s, scientist Robert Boyle and, even the great Sir Isaac Newton, believed that the goal of alchemy could be realized. Newton spent thousands of hours trying to make gold in his smoky laboratory, and he wrote a million words about his alchemical experiments. He actually spent more time on alchemy than he did making his revolutionary discoveries in physics and optics. It would take a major advance in chemical knowledge before it became clear why alchemy was impossible.

This sixteenth-century painting by
*Giovanni Stradano shows a busy community of alchemists
under the tutelage of a master (wearing spectacles and a cap).*

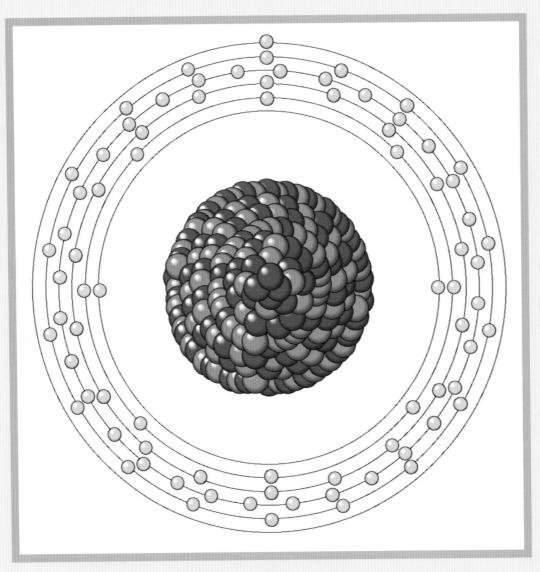

We know that gold consists of one kind of atom—
an atom composed of a nucleus of 79 protons and 118 neutrons encircled by
79 electrons arranged in 6 shells.

CHAPTER FOUR

What Is Gold?

THE END OF ALCHEMY

Alchemists tried to make gold for 2,000 years and never, in all that time, created the smallest fleck. No alchemist ever could have made gold because gold is a chemical element. Today, we define a chemical element as a substance made entirely of one kind of atom. One kind of atom cannot be changed by chemical means into another kind of atom. Elements cannot be created by adding the atoms of other substances together.

Remember that the ancient Greeks also used the word "element," but they defined the word differently than we do. They believed there were four elements: earth, air, fire, and water. The Greek definition of the four elements led alchemists to think they could create gold if they just combined the right amounts of earth, air, fire, and water in the right way.

The ancient Greeks' ideas about matter, including gold, were widespread and long-lasting. They passed from Greece to the Roman Empire and became a part of Christian beliefs through the Middle Ages. Until the 1600s, no one seriously

When the element sodium (whose standard abbreviation is Na) is combined with the element chlorine (abbreviated as Cl), a compound (NaCl) results. Water (H_2O) can be made by combining the elements of hydrogen (H) and oxygen (O). Salt and water are called compounds. They can be separated into two or more simpler substances by chemical means. Gold (Au) cannot be divided into any simpler substances.

questioned the idea that all matter, including gold, was composed of earth, air, fire, and water.

In the 1600s a number of scientists, including Robert Boyle, Robert Hooke, and John Mayow, began to explore the nature of matter. They used a new approach to understanding the natural world. Instead of forming an understanding of the world by simply observing it, as Aristotle and other ancient Greeks had done, these scientists used what would become known as the scientific method. The scientific method involves performing and repeating careful experiments, recording relevant data such as the weight and volume of substances, and forming hypotheses from the data.

Boyle, Hooke, and Mayow applied this new method to understanding air, one of the ancient Greek elements. They discovered that air was a more complex substance than the ancient Greeks had thought. Scientists in the 1700s continued to experiment with air. Joseph Black discovered carbon dioxide, Joseph Priestley isolated oxygen, and Henry Cavendish discovered hydrogen. The influence of Aristotle's ideas was so strong, though, that these scientists concluded that the gases they found were just varieties of the element air.

In 1783 the French chemist Antoine Lavoisier experimented with another of the Greek elements, water. He ran steam through a red-hot gun barrel and at the other end collected hydrogen gas and iron oxide. (Iron oxide is rust, which in this case formed when oxygen in the water combined with iron in the gun). It became clear to Lavoisier that water was made of at least two substances. He concluded that water could not, therefore, be an element.

Building on the experiments of Black, Priestley, and Cavendish, Lavoisier announced that air was not an element either. Oxygen was not, he declared, a kind of air; it was a separate substance *in* air. (Lavoisier was right: Air is actually a mixture of oxygen, nitrogen, and minute quantities of many other gaseous elements.) By proving that air and water were not elements, Lavoisier proved that the ancient Greek ideas about matter were wrong.

Lavoisier redefined the word "element." Now element meant a substance that could not be further divided by chemical means. Over the course of the two hundred years following Lavoisier's identification of oxygen, chemists have identified an additional one hundred elements, including gold, and brought us to our current understanding of matter.

GOLD AS AN ELEMENT

To understand more about the interactions among elements, scientists had to look further into their nature. At the center (called the nucleus) of any atom is a cluster of particles called protons. The protons have a positive (+) electrical charge. Mixed in with the protons in the nucleus are neutrons, particles that are similar in size to protons but have no electrical

Antoine Lavoisier
in his laboratory

charge. Whizzing around the nucleus are electrons, which have a negative (–) charge. (Particles with opposite charges attract each other. That's why electrons don't whiz off into space: They are attracted by the positively charged protons.) In an electrically neutral atom, the number of electrons is identical to the number of its protons.

If gold can't be made, how did it, or any other element, come into being? According to the latest theories, hydrogen and helium (which have one and two protons, respectively) were produced in the Big Bang when the universe was created. Those elements came together to form stars, like our sun. Other elements with a relatively small number of protons, like sodium (11 protons) and iron (26 protons), were made when the tremendous heat inside stars fused hydrogen and helium atoms together.

Physicists think that elements with very large numbers of protons, like gold with 79, were formed as large stars collapsed as they ran out of atomic fuel. As they collapsed, they generated huge gravitational pressures. Only under those pressures could the heavier atoms have formed. These elements were blasted out from such collapsing stars. When Earth formed from coalescing materials in space, gold became part of Earth.

Atomic particles—protons, neutrons, and electrons—are identical no matter what element they are in. What makes gold atoms different from oxygen atoms is the number of protons and neutrons they have in their nuclei. Oxygen, for example, has eight protons and eight neutrons in its nucleus. Gold has 79 protons and 118 neutrons in its nucleus.

Gold is often weighed in "troy ounces" and "troy pounds." These *troy weights* are slightly different than the usual avoirdupois ounces and pounds. One troy ounce is about 10 percent heavier than an avoirdupois ounce. There are twelve troy ounces in a troy pound, so a troy pound is about 82 percent of an avoirdupois pound.

Protons and neutrons are about two thousand times heavier than electrons. Because gold has so many particles in its nucleus, it is one of the heaviest elements. Of the elements that we commonly see, only lead and mercury are heavier. Remember how Alexander the Great's soldiers looted gold from Persia in 334–331 B.C.? Some of the soldiers buried their treasure along the trail when they left Persia, and no wonder. Marching thousands of miles with loot made of a metal as heavy as gold would have been no picnic!

Protons and neutrons make up most of the mass of an atom, but it is the electrons that determine how any atom will interact with other atoms. The number and arrangement of electrons around the nucleus determine an element's chemical behavior.

Electrons circle the nucleus of an atom at several specific distances from the nucleus. You can imagine that a nucleus has layers of shells around it, with electrons zooming around on the surfaces of those shells. Each shell has room for a particular number of electrons. Electrons fill the shells, starting with the innermost one and continuing out. Gold has six shells with its 79 electrons. (See diagram on page 48.)

Seventy-eight electrons fill the first five shells. The outermost shell has only one electron. This lonely electron in gold's outer shell is very important to the properties of gold. Because the single electron in the outermost shell of a gold atom is far from the nucleus, its attraction to the nucleus is not strong. Under certain circumstances, it will break free.

Gold atoms, as well as the atoms of other metals, stick closely together in regular, three-dimensional structures called lattices. (Whether the gold is formed into a gold wire or a gold brick, gold atoms arrange themselves in lattices.) In a lattice, the single electrons in the outermost shells often break free because they are pulled by the positive charges of the protons in neighboring gold atoms. These free electrons pass readily among the gold atoms in the lattice.

THE PROPERTIES OF GOLD

When any area of gold has a positive charge, the free electrons rush toward that area. When any area of the gold has a negative charge, the free electrons rush away from that area. When you apply electricity—which is a flow of electrons—to gold, the free electrons in the gold rush away from it, making electricity flow through the gold. You may know that silicon chips in the circuit boards of computers are connected by thin gold wires. Now you know why. Because gold's electrons move easily, gold conducts electricity very well.

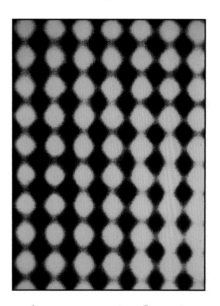

An atomic lattice of a thin gold crystal. Each yellow spot represents a single gold atom—magnified sixteen million times!

Your thumb is about 2 inches (5 centimeters) long. Imagine a cube of gold that is 2 inches (5 centimeters) on all sides. Take a look at a 5-pound (2.5-kilogram) bag of sugar the next time you're in the grocery store. The little gold cube and the bag of sugar weigh about the same! A standard gold brick in Fort Knox is the size of three candy bars stacked up, but it weighs 30 pounds (13.6 kilograms).

The free electrons in gold also give gold its luster. The free electrons race around among the gold atoms in a kind of cloud. When light shines on gold, the electron cloud reflects the light, so gold looks shiny to us.

The atomic structure of gold also explains why it is heavy. Metals, including gold, are close-packed. That means they fit as many atoms as possible into the space available. Imagine a layer of marbles covering the bottom of a box. Then imagine putting a second layer on top of the first. The bottoms of the marbles in the second layer will fit snugly into the intersections of the marbles in the first layer. A third layer of marbles will fit neatly into the intersections of the second layer. This is the way gold atoms fit together, and there is no way to pack atoms (or marbles) more tightly into a given space.

So gold is heavy for two reasons: Individual gold atoms are heavy because their nuclei contain 79 protons and 118 neutrons. Also, gold atoms are close-packed, so more atoms of gold fit into the same volume of space than the atoms of many other elements.

Gold is also very malleable (easy to shape). It can be stretched into long threads and hammered flat into the thinnest of sheets. These qualities make gold an ideal material for jewelry and for gilding church domes.

A sheet
of gold foil

Why is gold so malleable? To see the answer, keep your layers of marbles in mind. Then add to your mental picture a cloud of shared electrons enveloping the gold atoms on all sides and between the layers. The electron cloud acts like a strong glue to hold the atoms of gold together. But while the cloud holds the marbles together, you can also see that the layers of marbles could quite easily slide across each other. That's just what happens in gold: Layers of gold atoms slip easily past one another, while a glue of electrons holds the atoms together. That's why gold is easy to pull into a wire or hammer into a thin sheet.

Once chemists understood the structure of gold and other elements, they understood the reasons for gold's seemingly magical qualities. It is gold's atomic structure that makes it durable, shiny, heavy yet malleable . . . and impossible to manufacture. Chemistry spelled the end of alchemy.

An ounce of gold—about the size of a piece of bubble gum—can be stretched into a wire 50 miles (80 kilometers) long. You could hammer three candy-bar-sized pieces of gold into a thin sheet that would cover a football field.

On display are gold shavings, bricks, and bars
from a modern-day vault.

CHAPTER FIVE

Gold, Ancient and Modern

In the eighth century B.C., the ancient Lydians produced the first government-issued, uniform gold coins. People in the region recognized the coins and trusted that the Lydian government had made them all an identical weight. Lydian coins became a popular means to pay for goods and services. In the succeeding centuries, the Persians and the Greeks minted their own gold coins, and these coins, too, became accepted currency.

By about A.D. 200, the Roman Empire encompassed all of Western Europe, modern England, the north coast of Africa, and much of the Middle East. The Roman government needed a great deal of gold to pay its many and far-flung mercenary soldiers to keep them loyal. The Roman government also paid in gold coins for the bread bought from abroad to feed the Roman people. In this way, Roman gold coins—called *bezants*—circulated across the huge empire and even beyond, as far as China.

The more widely that gold coins were accepted, the greater the demand was for gold to mint more coins. As the Romans exhausted the gold mines of Italy, Gaul (modern France), and Spain, they conquered new lands in the Balkans (north of Greece) to gain access to new gold mines. Even then, the supply of gold was not large enough to meet Rome's needs. When the emperor Constantine made Christianity the state religion in A.D. 313, he stripped all the pagan temples in the empire of their gold images and furnishings, melted them down, and minted the gold into bezants.

By the Middle Ages, the gold mines in Europe were exhausted, and there was little new gold reaching Europe. (The Arabs were producing new gold from their mines in West Africa and Egypt, but there was little commerce between the Arabs and Europeans.) In fact, Europe's gold supply was shrinking. Some of Europe's gold went to the Far East to pay for the spices and silks that Europeans liked. Some went to the bottom of the sea when trading ships sank. Some was squirreled away by people hoarding the increasingly rare metal. In Europe, gold became too scarce to use for day-to-day payments like buying cloth or milk. Silver—trading for gold at a ratio of about ten to one—filled the need.

When the English had to pay a ransom for the return of Richard the Lion Hearted (the King Richard of the Robin Hood stories) in about A.D. 1200, they paid with 24 million silver pennies!

NEW SUPPLIES OF GOLD

The need for new sources of gold inspired, in part, the great European voyages of discovery in the fifteenth, sixteenth, and seventeenth centuries. The Portuguese were the first to reap a golden benefit from their adventures. They ventured south into the forbidding Atlantic Ocean in the 1400s, armed with their compasses and new maps, and sailed down the west coast of Africa. They set up trading posts in North Africa and West Africa (modern Ghana), where they could profit from trading for gold, as well as spices and slaves.

When Columbus landed in Hispaniola (the island in the Caribbean that the Dominican Republic and Haiti share today) in 1493, he and his men immediately looked for gold. The Spanish conquered large areas of Latin America in the sixteenth century, largely in their quest to find gold. From 1500 to 1600, Spanish fleets carried away about 750,000 pounds (340,000 kilograms) of

In the land of the Incas (modern Peru) in 1532, Spanish conquistador Francisco Pizarro thought he'd found *El Dorado*, the legendary land of gold. When Pizarro and his soldiers arrived, Atahualpa, king of the Inca Empire, welcomed them to his kingdom. Pizarro repaid his friendliness by murdering two thousand unarmed and terrified Incas. He then captured Atahualpa and demanded a room full of gold as ransom for the king's release. Inca peasants provided six tons of gold, all in the form of their beautiful ornaments, jewelry, and small art objects. Although the Incas fulfilled Pizarro's demand for ransom, Pizarro backed out of his part of the bargain and publicly strangled Atahualpa. He then melted down the ransom, destroying centuries' worth of Incan art.

This Peruvian gold mask was made around A.D. 1400.

gold from Latin America, mostly from Peru and Mexico, to Europe.

In 1695 the Portuguese discovered an even larger source of gold in Brazil. The world's first popular gold rush was on. (Previous gold discoveries had been controlled and exploited by emperors or kings.) People from all over the world poured into Brazil, hoping to make their fortunes. They brought tens of thousands of African slaves to do the actual mining, many of whom died in the horrific conditions in the mines.

The first gold in North America was found by the son of a German-born farmer in North Carolina in 1799. John Reed (formerly known as Johannes Reith) had settled in the Piedmont region of North Carolina at the end of the Revolutionary War. One Sunday, Reed's son Conrad brought home an unusual, baseball-sized rock he'd found in a creek. The Reed family used the rock as a doorstop for three years, until a Fayetteville jeweler identified it as a 17-pound (7.7-kilogram) gold nugget! This revelation sparked another gold rush. The Piedmont mountain area of North Carolina produced all the gold for the U.S. Mint in Philadelphia until 1828.

Vast new deposits of gold were found in California in 1848, in Australia in 1850, in Canada in 1858, and in the Canadian and American Yukon in the late 1890s. These gold strikes brought hordes of gold prospectors from around the globe, pick and pan in hand, to scratch or shake gold from dirt or sand. (More than a million people went to Australia in search of gold.) Once prospectors had removed the gold found near

A tinted photograph of miners panning
for gold in the Klondike, 1897

the surface and from streams, mining companies, with the costly equipment required for deeper mining, took over.

Many miners arrived in the American West and in western Canada. They expected to scoop up a fortune quickly and easily, but most were badly disappointed. It didn't take long for the easy pickings to be picked. By the time the great waves of prospectors arrived, there was little easy gold to be found. In the Yukon, prospectors discovered they had to melt up to 30 feet (9 meters) of permafrost before they could begin to dig into potentially gold-bearing gravel.

The greatest modern gold deposits of all were found in South Africa in 1885 by an Australian handyman named George Harrison. Harrison was cutting stones from the rocky earth near Johannesburg to build a house when he came across gold. It turned out he had cut into a *gold reef* (a layer of gold) that ultimately proved to be part of an arc of reefs about 300 miles (483 kilometers) long. These reefs, constantly mined

A miner operates a powerful drill to blast away the rock face inside a South African gold mine.

since 1885, contain the world's largest known deposits of gold, and they produce more than half of the world's gold today.

Some individual mines in South Africa produce more gold than all the mines of Canada and the United States (the world's second- and third-largest gold producers) combined. The mines of South Africa are extraordinarily deep, though, and the gold is distributed in minute particles among huge quantities of rock. These factors make South African gold very expensive to mine. About 6 tons of rock must be blasted out and carried up as much as 2 miles (3 kilometers) to the surface in order to recover about 1 ounce (28 grams) of gold.

Fortunately for the South African gold industry, in 1887 a Scottish chemist named John Stewart MacArthur invented the *cyanide process* for unlocking the tiny amounts of gold contained in the South African ore. Once the ore was crushed to the texture of powder, a chemical solution containing cyanide was added to dissolve the gold. The gold in the solution was then separated from the cyanide by adding zinc dust, which combined with the cyanide. A variation of MacArthur's process is still used today.

GOLD AND PAPER CURRENCY

The discoveries of great amounts of gold in the nineteenth century meant there was a lot more gold available for people to use to buy and sell things and to accumulate as savings. Gold became firmly reestablished as the ideal substance to use as currency.

It wasn't always practical, however, to pass gold back and

forth between buyers and sellers. As far back as 1700 in England, some people had taken their money to private banks and to goldsmiths where they put their gold "on deposit." The bank then issued a paper banknote or the goldsmith issued a paper receipt for the gold deposit. The issuer promised, in writing, to pay that amount in gold whenever the holder of the banknote or receipt presented the paper for exchange. In this way, banknotes and receipts, instead of the actual metal, could be exchanged among buyers, sellers, and traders. This system worked because people were confident that they could exchange these pieces of paper for precious metal at any time.

Private banks and individual goldsmiths usually upheld their part of the bargain, but not always. Bankers might accept deposits of gold, issue notes, and then use the gold for other purposes (such as investing or lending with interest). They would estimate how much gold they needed to keep in the vault in order to pay note holders who might arrive to collect their gold. From time to time, bankers guessed incorrectly. Note holders would arrive to retrieve their gold only to discover that the bank didn't have enough gold in its vaults to pay them. Then the bank would fail, and the owners of the gold would lose their deposits.

In the nineteenth century, as the world's stock of gold grew, Britain, other European countries, and the United States organized national banks that took deposits and guaranteed that gold would be available to note holders. For a period of roughly fifty years, from the 1870s through the 1930s, many of the world's economies operated on the international gold standard, which meant that the national banks were prepared to exchange paper currencies for gold in any amount and at any time. As one economist, Robert Mundell, put it: Under the international gold standard, "Currencies were just names for particular weights of gold."

During the worldwide economic slump of the 1930s, called the Great Depression, many countries had to go off the gold standard. The prices of all goods, from butter to gold, were falling because people were out of work or had lost their savings in bank failures, so they couldn't afford to buy things. People first lost confidence in the British economy and took their pound notes to the Bank of England to exchange for gold. Soon, so much gold had left the Bank of England that Britain announced it would no longer provide gold on demand. That meant Britain was off the gold standard. Within days, twenty-four other countries—about half the countries on the gold standard—followed suit. Gold was no longer money.

THE VALUE OF GOLD TODAY

Today, you can't pay for your groceries in gold, and you can't walk into a bank and routinely exchange your paper currency for gold. Still, gold is very valuable: In September 2002, gold was selling for about $323 an ounce. Millions of people all over the world, especially in Asia, continue to use gold as a basic form of savings.

People liked the gold standard system because values of currencies didn't change in relation to gold or to each other. For example, one dollar was worth 23.22 grains of gold and one British pound was worth 113.0016 grains of gold. (A *grain* is the smallest unit of weight in the U.S. and British systems.) This meant that one British pound was always worth exactly $4.86 (113.0016 grains ÷ 23.22 grains).

Gold is still highly valued in jewelry. Because gold is beautiful and durable, it continues to be a popular material for wedding bands, bracelets, and necklaces. In recent years, about three thousand tons of gold have been used in jewelry annually. Modern artists, too, continue to use gold. Church and mosque domes are still gilded with thin layers of gold. Each year, many thousands of pounds of gold are used for decorative purposes.

Adorned with gold, the Dome of the Rock in Jerusalem is a striking example of gold used in architecture.

An extra-ordinary gold necklace and earring bridal ensemble, modeled by an Indian actress in a Bombay, India, jewelry shop

Detail of a space shuttle astronaut's gold-coated helmet visor

Today, gold is valued as much for its physical properties as for its beauty. When astronauts walked on the moon, they wore helmets with visors coated in gold because gold reflects up to 99 percent of infrared rays. Because gold is also an excellent conductor of heat, gold is used in the engine of the space shuttle. Temperatures in the shuttle's engine can reach above

5,432°F (3,000°C), and gold efficiently channels that heat away from delicate instruments in the engine.

As you saw in Chapter Four, gold conducts electricity very well. Even a tiny charge flows easily through it. As a result, the electronics industry uses gold to make the miniature electrical contacts and wires found in computers and other electronic devices. In 1999 about 240 tons of gold went into making billions of electrical contacts.

Dentists around the world use more than 65 tons of gold every year to make fillings for teeth and other dental uses. They use gold because it is so easy to shape to fill all the space left by a cavity. Less malleable materials can leave a space where bacteria can collect and cause further damage. Dentists use gold, too, because it doesn't rust or otherwise deteriorate.

More than six thousand years ago, the ancient Egyptian rulers found that gold could be a blazing symbol of power and authority, as well as an expression of beauty. About five thousand years ago, the Mesopotamians discovered that the beautiful metal was also an excellent way to store wealth and to make trade easier. We still appreciate gold's beauty, but today our rulers no longer wear gold crowns or dress in cloth of gold. We're more likely to store our wealth in bank accounts or stocks than gold bars, and we use paper currency, not gold coins, to trade for goods and services. The one characteristic of gold that our ancestors never appreciated—its usefulness as a material in industry and technology—is now what we value most about it!

SCOTLAND

SCANDINAVIA

GREAT BRITAIN

HOLLAND

IRELAND   ENGLAND

London

GERMANY

EUROPE

R U S

ATLANTIC

Paris

OCEAN

GAUL

FRANCE   ALPS

Danube R.

ITALY

Rome

PORTUGAL

Iberian Peninsula

Mt. Olympus

THRACE

MACEDON

BLACK SEA

CAUCASUS

Colchis

Constantinople (Istanbul)

MYCENAE

PHRYGIA

LYDIA (TURKEY)

ASSYRIA

MEDITERRANEAN SEA

Athens

Karpathos

King Midas's
Tomb

MESOPOTAMIA

Cala

SUMER

ATLAS MTNS.

Crete
(Minoan
Kingdom)

Cyprus

SYRIA

ISRAEL

Euphrates R.

Tigris

Baghdad

BABYLON

Alexandria

Jerusalem

King Solomon's
Temple

Memphis
(Cairo)

SAHARA DESERT

EGYPT

ARABIA

ARABIAN
DESERT

Mecca

Nile R.

RED SEA

A F R I C A

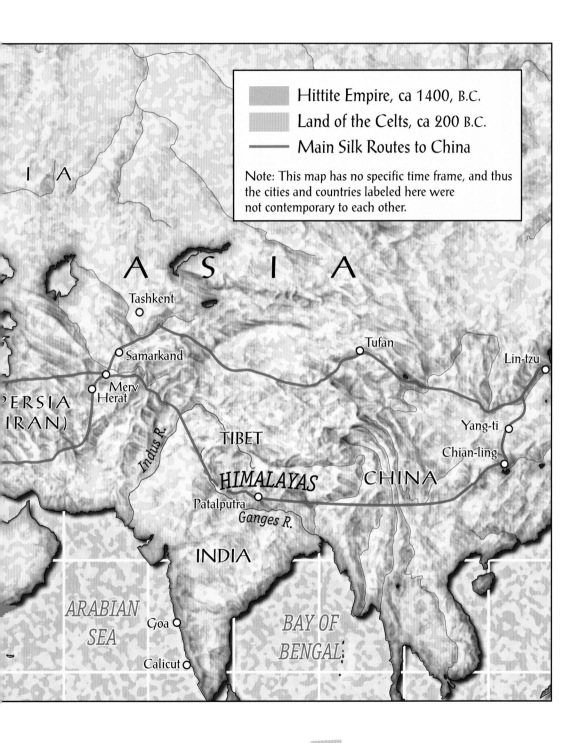

Hittite Empire, ca 1400, B.C.

Land of the Celts, ca 200 B.C.

Main Silk Routes to China

Note: This map has no specific time frame, and thus the cities and countries labeled here were not contemporary to each other.

I A

A S I A

Tashkent

Tufan

Samarkand

Lin-tzu

Merv
Herat

(PERSIA
(IRAN)

Yang-ti

Indus R.

Chian-ling

TIBET

HIMALAYAS

CHINA

Patalputra

Ganges R.

INDIA

ARABIAN
SEA

Goa

BAY OF
BENGAL

Calicut

Timeline

B.C.

4500–3000	Egyptians begin panning for gold
1300	King Tut is buried with gold treasures
1000	King Solomon's gilded temple is built; people begin to use gold as currency
600	Individuals are forbidden to make their own coins for trade; Lydian government issues standard coinage
546	Persia invades Lydia and adopts the idea of gold as currency, establishing a government mint
334–331	Alexander the Great's armies conquer Persia and loot its gold, spreading the idea of gold as the perfect metal
315	Emperor Constantine forbids the study of alchemy in the Roman Empire

A.D.

200	Roman Empire mints bezants; coins circulate as far as China
1100	Idea of alchemy spreads to Europe; it becomes acceptable to practice as a profession
1400s	Portuguese travel to North and West Africa to trade with natives for gold, spices, and slaves
1600s	Scientists discover that gold is an element
1695	Portuguese discover large source of gold in Brazil
1799	First discovery of gold in North America—Conrad Reed finds a 17-pound gold nugget in a North Carolina creek
1828	Georgia has America's first gold rush
1848	California gold rush begins
1873	Dollars as currency can be exchanged with gold or silver
1968	United States no longer uses the gold standard
1969	Astronauts walk on the moon, wearing gilded helmets to deflect the light; gold is also used to conduct heat in the space shuttle engine
Late 1900s	Gold becomes valuable for its various uses in electronic devices

Glossary

alchemy: the would-be science of turning base metals to gold

aqua regia: a liquid composed of nitric acid and hydrochloric acid that is able to dissolve gold

bezant: a gold coin of the Byzantine Empire widely circulated in the Middle Ages

cupel: a small cuplike container used to separate gold or silver from lead

cupellation: the process of separating gold or silver from lead by heating substances in a cupel

cyanide process: a chemical process for separating gold from ore

dumps: small bean-shaped bits of electrum formed into regular shapes by the goldsmiths of ancient Sardis

electrum: an alloy of gold and silver

filigree: decorations made of tiny gold wires twisted and bent into fanciful, lacy designs

gild: to coat with gold

gold-electroplated: coated with gold

gold-filled: made of a base metal to which a layer of gold has been bonded

gold foil: thin gold used for gilding objects

gold-plated: coated with gold

gold reef: a layer of gold in the Earth

goldsmithing: making objects out of gold

grain: the smallest unit of weight in the U.S. and British systems of measurement

granulation: soldering tiny spheres of gold onto gold surfaces as decoration

international gold standard: a monetary system in which a unit of gold is the accepted unit of value

karat: a unit for measuring and identifying the purity of gold

mint: a place where coins and paper currency are produced under the authority of a government

nub: the ancient Egyptian word for gold

repoussé: technique of raising an area of the surface of a thin sheet of gold by pushing it from underneath

touchstone: a black stone used to test the purity of gold

troy weight: a system of weights used for precious metals and gems

BOOKS

Aesop. *The Aesop for Children*. New York: Scholastic, 1994.

Baum, L. Frank. *The Wizard of Oz*. New York: Alfred A. Knopf, 1900.

Bernstein, Peter. *The Story of Gold: The History of an Obsession*. New York: John Wiley, 2000.

Cobb, Cathy, and Harold Goldwhite. *Creations of Fire: Chemistry's Lively History from Alchemy to the Atomic Age*. Norwell, MA: Plenum Press, 1995.

Edwards, I.E.S. *Tutankhamen: His Tomb and Its Treasures*. New York: Alfred A. Knopf, 1976.

Graves, Robert. *The Greek Myths*. New York: Penguin, 1992.

Hellman, Hal. *The Story of Gold*. Danbury, CT: Franklin Watts, 1996.

Maestro, Betsy. *The Story of Money*. New York: Clarion, 1993.

Meltzer, Milton. *Gold: The True Story of Why People Search for It, Mine It, Trade It, Steal It, Mint It, Hoard It, Shape It, Wear It, Fight and Kill for It*. New York: HarperCollins, 1993.

Philip, Neil. *Odin's Family: The Myths of the Vikings*. New York: Orchard Books, 1996.

INTERNET RESOURCES

Chamber of Mines of South Africa
www.bullion.org.za

The Gold Institute
www.goldinstitute.org

Encyclopedia Mythica
www.pantheon.org

Index